First Facts®

Christmas around the World

Christmas in
NORWAY

by Jack Manning

CAPSTONE PRESS
a capstone imprint

First Facts are published by Capstone Press,
1710 Roe Crest Drive, North Mankato, Minnesota 56003
www.capstonepub.com

Library of Congress Cataloging-in-Publication Data
Manning, Jack.
  Christmas in Norway / by Jack Manning.
    pages cm.—(First facts: Christmas around the world)
  Includes index.
  ISBN 978-1-4765-3101-4 (library binding)
  ISBN 978-1-4765-3432-9 (ebook PDF)
1. Christmas—Norway—Juvenile literature. 2. Norway—Social life and customs—Juvenile
literature. I. Title.
  GT4987.59.M36 2014
  394.2663—dc23
                                                          2013003259

Editorial Credits
Brenda Haugen, editor; Gene Bentdahl, designer; Eric Gohl, media researcher;
Jennifer Walker, production specialist

Photo Credits
Alamy: Arctic Photo, 1; Art Directors & Trip: Gv Press, 17; Capstone Studio: Karon Dubke, 6, 8,
12, 18, 21; Corbis: Atlantide Phototravel, cover; iStockphotos: Ekely, 11; Newscom: ZUMA Press/
Rabouan Jean-Baptiste, 5; Rex USA: Francis Dean, 15

Design Elements: Shutterstock

Printed in China by Nordica.
0314/CA21400180
022014   007226NORDF13

TABLE OF CONTENTS

Christmas in Norway

Church bells ring in the cold winter air. Pretty paper chains and heart-shaped baskets decorate many homes. Families join hands and walk around their Christmas trees. It is Christmas in Norway! People in Norway celebrate with gifts and **traditional** music and food.

traditional—handed down from one generation to another within a family or culture

Norway

How to Say It!
In Norway people say *"God Jul"* (GOH YUHL),
which means "Good Christmas."

CHRISTMAS FACT!

Three kings followed a bright star to find the baby Jesus. The kings brought gifts for him.

The First Christmas

On Christmas, **Christians** celebrate the birth of **Jesus**. Long ago Jesus' parents, Mary and Joseph, traveled to Bethlehem. The Middle Eastern city was crowded. Mary and Joseph could not find a place to stay. Finally they found shelter in a stable. That night Jesus was born.

Christian—a person who follows a religion based on the teachings of Jesus
Jesus—the founder of the Christian religion

Christmas Celebrations

Many Norwegians celebrate Little Christmas Eve on December 23. As their children sleep, parents carry Christmas trees into their homes. In the morning the children see the decorated trees. Sometimes they find presents under the trees.

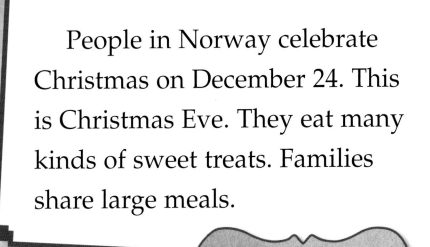

People in Norway celebrate Christmas on December 24. This is Christmas Eve. They eat many kinds of sweet treats. Families share large meals.

CHRISTMAS FACT!

Most Norwegians also celebrate Saint Lucia Day on December 13. Saint Lucia was a Christian who often brought food to the hungry.

Christmas Symbols

Juleneks (YUH-le-neks) are symbols of Christmas in Norway. A julenek is made from stalks of grain. It is often tied to a tree branch, pole, or railing. People believe it is good luck if birds eat the grain. Some people clear a circle of snow below each julenek. They believe that birds dance in the circle before eating.

CHRISTMAS FACT!

Some people decorate Christmas trees with glass balls and candles. Others use pinecones and fake birds as decorations.

Christmas Decorations

Many people make their decorations. Some create heart-shaped baskets. Children make long, colorful paper chains. Families often put the chains on their Christmas trees.

People often decorate their homes with things found in nature. They put branches, pinecones, and pieces of straw in bowls or baskets.

Santa Claus

Julenissen (YUH-le-ni-sen) brings joy to children in Norway. He is a mix of Santa Claus and an elf called the *nisse* (NI-se). Julenissen has a long, white beard and wears a red cap. He carries gifts to children's homes in a sack on his back.

CHRISTMAS FACT!

On Christmas Eve some people leave a bowl of **porridge** for the nisse. They believe the elf protects people who work hard.

porridge—a creamy, hot cereal

15

Christmas Presents

Children often find their gifts under the Christmas tree. Others find their gifts on the tree! Parents may tie small presents to the tree's lower branches.

So what do children get for Christmas? Some receive toys, books, and games. Others get skis, sleds, or skates. Mittens, hats, scarves, and sweaters are favorite presents too.

lefse

Christmas Food

Homes are filled with many amazing smells on Christmas Eve. Most people eat pork and boiled potatoes for their evening meal. The steaming vegetable with the green or purple leaves is sweet and sour cabbage.

Some people eat lutefisk (LOO-te-fisk). This traditional dish is codfish that is soaked in a liquid called lye. The fish is then baked.

Many people enjoy sweet treats too. *Julekake* (YUH-le-kah-ke) is a sweet bread with raisins. Lefse (LEF-se) is a flat, sweetened bread. People usually eat lefse with butter and sugar.

CHRISTMAS FACT!

People often bake several kinds of cookies at Christmastime. They offer these treats to guests who drop by.

Christmas Songs

The sounds of music and church bells fill the air. It's Christmastime in Norway!

Many families sing while holding hands and walking around their Christmas trees. Small families hold stuffed animals and dolls between them. This makes the circle big enough to reach around the tree.

People sometimes sing around trees at church or at work. If there are lots of singers, they may form many rings around the trees.

CHRISTMAS FACT!

Church bells ring throughout Norway at 5 p.m. on December 24. This lets people know that Christmas Eve is starting.

Hands-On:

MAKE A JULENEK

People in Norway make juleneks as Christmas treats for the birds. Make your own julenek and see if birds come to dance around it. Your julenek may bring you good luck too!

What You Need

- 1-yard-long (91-centimeter-long) branch or stick
- several stalks of grain
- string
- brightly colored ribbon

What You Do

1. Surround the branch with stalks of grain.
2. Tie the string around the branch and stalks. Make sure to tie it tightly.
3. Tie the ribbon around the string as a decoration.
4. Use string to tie the julenek to a railing or pole. Try to put the julenek somewhere that is easy to see. Then you can watch out the window as birds eat the grain.

GLOSSARY

Christian (KRIS-chuhn)—a person who follows a religion based on the teachings of Jesus

Jesus (JEE-zuhs)—the founder of the Christian religion

porridge (POR-ij)—a creamy, hot cereal

traditional (truh-DISH-uh-nul)—handed down from one generation to another within a family or culture

READ MORE

Kopka, Deborah L. *Norway.* Country Explorers.
Minneapolis: Lerner Publications, 2010.

Trunkhill, Brenda. *Christmas Around the World.*
St. Louis: Concordia Publishing House, 2009.

Zobel, Derek. *Norway.* Exploring Countries.
Minneapolis: Bellwether Media, 2012.

INTERNET SITES

FactHound offers a safe, fun way to find Internet sites related to this book. All of the sites on FactHound have been researched by our staff.

Here's all you do:

Visit *www.facthound.com*

Type in this code: 9781476531014

Check out projects, games and lots more at
www.capstonekids.com

23

INDEX